MW00583886

DUMP TRUCKS

by Judith Jango-Cohen
photographs by Judith Jango-Cohen and Eliot Cohen

Lerner Publications Company • Minneapolis

A special thank you is due to Stephen Ward, Margaret McInnis, and all the drivers at Benevento Sand and Stone. Thanks also to Ray MacDonald and Walter Palladino at Quinn-Perkins Sand and Gravel, and to Peter Shinney for the exciting ride. —J.J.C.

Dedicated to Eloise Orsini, Burlington kindergarten teacher, whose students write beautiful books and who encouraged my writing from the start. —J.J.C.

This book is available in two editions:
Library binding by Lerner Publications Company, a division of Lerner Publishing Group
Soft cover by First Avenue Editions, an imprint of Lerner Publishing Group
241 First Avenue North
Minneapolis, MN 55401 U.S.A.

Website address: www.lernerbooks.com

Library of Congress Cataloging-in-Publication Data

Jango-Cohen, Judith.
Dump trucks / by Judith Jango-Cohen; photographs by Judith Jango-Cohen and Eliot Cohen.
p. cm. — (Pull ahead books)
Includes index.
Summary: Introduces the functions and parts of dump trucks.
ISBN: 0–8225–0688–2 (lib. bdg. : alk. paper)
ISBN: 0–8225–0602–5 (pbk. : alk. paper)
1. Earthwork—Juvenile literature. 2. Dump trucks—Juvenile literature. [1. Dump trucks. 2. Trucks.]
I. Title. II. Series.
TA732 .J35 2003
629.225—dc21 2001006140

Manufactured in the United States of America
3 4 5 6 7 8 — JR — 09 08 07 06 05 04

How do you move a mountain?

Get a dump truck!

Dump trucks carry big **loads** from place to place. Then they dump the loads.

This truck is moving a load of snow.
The snowy load goes into the **bed**.

The driver rides inside the cab. Does the driver ever get into the bed?

This driver gets into the bed to cover his load. The cover keeps the snow from falling onto the road.

The driver pushes these **levers** to make his truck dump. What do the levers do?

Levers make **pistons** slide out. The pistons tip back the bed. The back of the truck opens up.

WHOOSH! Out slips the snow. This is how dump trucks dump. But how are they filled?

A **front-end loader** can fill a dump truck. This one picks up broken branches.

The front-end loader lifts the branches. They crack and crash into the dump truck's bed.

Dump trucks also work with diggers called **excavators**. Excavators dig holes with their spiky buckets.

The spikes rip into the dirt. CLUNK! CLANG! BANG! Dirt and rocks drop into the truck.

Dump trucks move branches and snow. They move dirt dug from holes. But some dump trucks help fill holes.

This truck is loaded with **asphalt.** Asphalt fills holes in roads. Do you know what the doors are for?

The driver
opens the
doors to let
hot asphalt
pour out.

Then the driver presses the hot asphalt into the hole.

Some dump trucks never go onto roads. They are too big.

This dump truck works at a pit where people dig up rock. The truck is so big that a ladder leads up to the cab.

The wheels of this truck are bigger than the driver.

The dump truck carries a load of big rocks. It rumbles up a dusty path.

The driver stops at the top of the path. He tips back the bed.

The load of big rocks drops into the **crusher**. The crusher crunches the rocks into smaller stones.

Now a
mountain
of crushed
stone must
be moved to
people who
are making
a road.

What luck! Here comes a dump truck.

Facts about Dump Trucks

- Dump trucks sometimes work at mines. They carry rocks filled with bits of gold, silver, and diamonds.
- If a dump truck is too big to be driven to a work site on roads, it is brought there in pieces. Workers put the truck together at the work site.
- Some dump trucks have lights that flash when the bed is almost full.
- One tire on a giant dump truck may weigh more than three cars.
- Some dump trucks have 18 wheels.

Parts of a Dump Truck

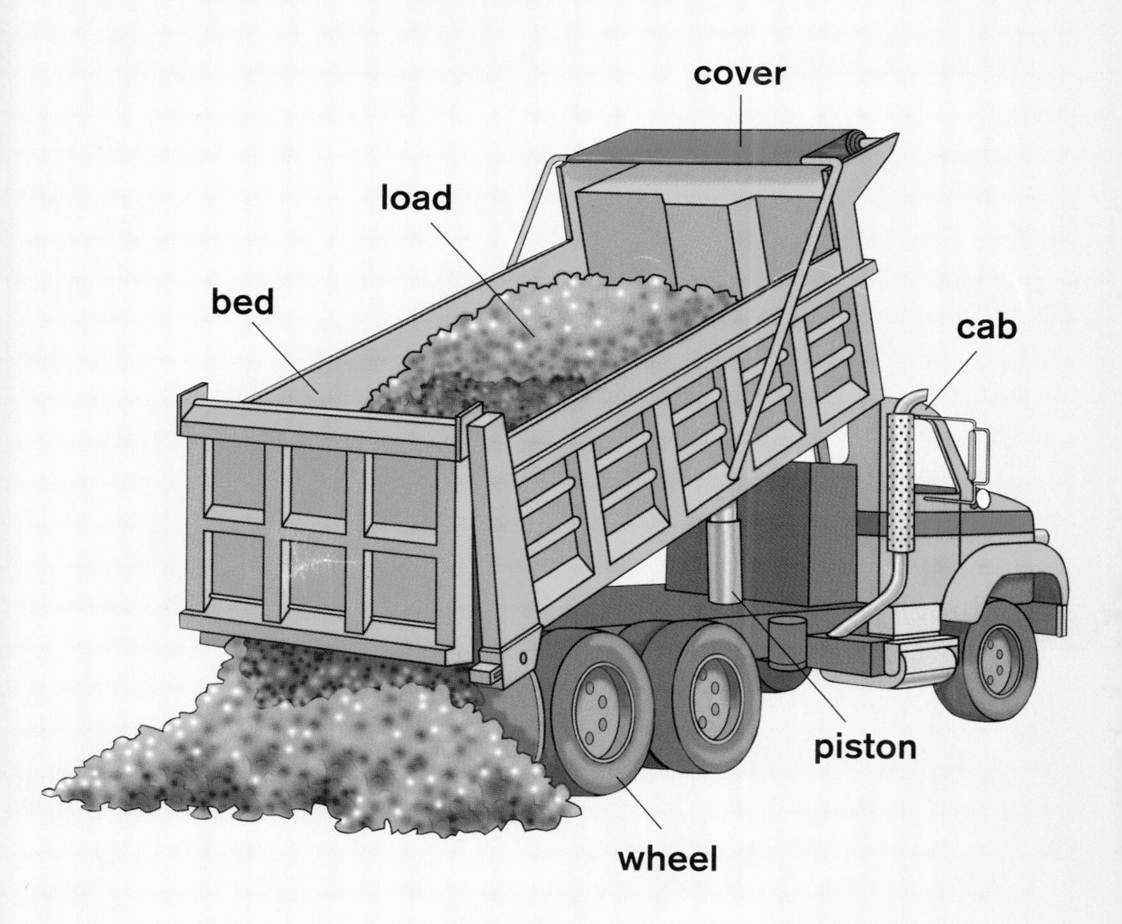

Glossary

asphalt: a black, sticky material used to make roads

bed: the back part of a dump truck where things are carried

crusher: a machine that breaks big rocks

excavators: large machines that dig holes

front-end loader: a machine with a shovel in front that scoops and pours

levers: controls that a driver pushes to make a dump truck dump

loads: the things that dump trucks carry

pistons: metal rods that push up the back of a dump truck so it can dump

Index

Eliot Cohen

About the Author

When Judith Jango-Cohen began looking for dump trucks to photograph and write about, she wasn't sure where she'd find them. But she soon discovered dump truck drivers helping out all over her hometown of Burlington, Massachusetts. The drivers were hauling away snow, filling holes in roads, carrying away broken tree limbs, and working at construction sites and quarries. Dump trucks are big, noisy, and exciting, and their drivers are very nice. One even let Judith ride in his cab. Look around for dump trucks in your neighborhood. You'll probably find them everywhere.

Photo Acknowledgments

Additional photographs courtesy of: © Dan Lamont/CORBIS, front cover, p. 21; © James L. Amos/CORBIS, back cover; © Charles O'Rear/CORBIS, p. 20; © Layne Kennedy/CORBIS, p. 22. Illustration on p. 29 by Laura Westlund, © Lerner Publications Company.